Exploring Cultures
in the Kitchen

French Culture and Cooking

Lindsey Lowe

Cavendish
Square

Children's Publisher: Anne O'Daly
Design Manager: Keith Davis
Picture Manager: Sophie Mortimer

Picture Credits
t=top, c=center, b=bottom, l=left, r=right
Front Cover: Shutterstock: Veniamin Kraskov br, Frederic Legrand tl, Timofeyeva Lyubov tr, Leena Robinson bl.
Interior: Dreamstime: Anizza 21, Artiomstorojenco 23, chandlervid85 10-11b, Peter Lovas 39, Juan Ignacio Polo 7t, Viachaslau Zhukau 20-21b; iStock: Bruby 38b, Jodie Chapman 30t, LuckyBusiness 1l, 36-37t; Shutterstock: 15b, 35b, 41b, 123pixels 8-9b, beboy 5t, Delpixel 30-31b, Elena Dijour 39, Pierre Jean Durieu 22-23, EBASCOL 38t, Anton Gvozdikov 5b, ilovecoffeedesign 20, Nigel Jarvis 9, Timofeyeva Lyubov 1r, 27bl, Margouilat Photo 25br, 45b, maziarz 36-37b, Mistervlad 6t, PHILIPIMAGE 8-9t, pukach 31t, pukao 19cr, Radu Razvan 22, Pedro Sala 11t, salajean 10t, Sea Wave 17b, travelpeter 6-7b, Didier Wuthrich 4l, Huang Zhen 38-39b; Thinkstock: istockphoto 43b.

Special thanks to Klaus Arras for all other photography.

Cataloging-in-Publication Data

Names: Lowe, Lindsey.
Title: French culture and cooking / Lindsey Lowe.
Description: Buffalo, New York: Cavendish Square Publishing, 2024. | Series: Exploring cultures in the kitchen | Includes glossary and index.
Identifiers: ISBN 9781502668981 (pbk.) | ISBN 9781502668998 (library bound) | ISBN 9781502669001 (ebook)
Subjects: LCSH: Cooking, French--Juvenile literature. | Food--France--Juvenile literature. | Food habits--France--Juvenile literature. | France--Social life and customs--Juvenile literature.
Classification: LCC TX719.O34 2024 | DDC 641.5944--dc23

CPSIA compliance information: Batch #CSCSQ24: For further information contact Cavendish Square Publishing LLC at 1-877-980-4450.

Printed in the United States of America

Find us on

Contents

Spotlight on France

France is one of the oldest nations on Earth. It is also the largest country in Western Europe. Rich in history and culture, France is famous for its delicious food!

EUROPE

France

AFRICA

France is bordered by the European countries of Spain, Belgium, Luxembourg, Germany, Switzerland, and Italy.

The crunchy baguette is the type of bread most commonly eaten by the French.

Long Live France!

People from all over the world live in France and feed into its dynamic culture. As well as its cuisine, France is famous for art, music, fashion, architecture, sports, and literature. Around 80 million tourists visit each year, soaking up the stylish fashion, great food, and amazing art. At the Louvre Museum in Paris, 10 million visitors per year view artist Leonardo da Vinci's *Mona Lisa*. However, it´s not just the cities that attract visitors. France´s landscape offers up a breathtaking range of scenery, from sunny beaches and harbors to stunning mountains and gentle plains farther inland. Vive la France (long live France)!

Paris is the capital of France. It lies on the Seine River in northern France. The Eiffel Tower is one of the city's famous landmarks.

NETHERLANDS

BELGIUM

Lille

ARDENNES

Seine

Mont Saint-Michel NORMANDY

BRITTANY

○ Paris

Strasbourg ○

Orléans

Loire

Loire

ATLANTIC
OCEAN

FRANCE

AUVERGNE

Lyon

Bordeaux

Garonne

Rhône

PROVENCE

AQUITAINE

Toulouse

PYRENEES

Marseilles

SPAIN

MEDITERRANEAN SEA

Provence is a region in southeastern France. It is famous for its bright purple lavender fields. Lavender has a strong fragrance and is used in perfumes and soaps.

Central France

The Auvergne region is an area of great natural beauty. Cyclists, nature lovers, and hikers flock to its regional parks and relax in its spring-fed spas, such as Vichy. In the east, the snowy French Alps mountain range attracts thousands of skiers during winter. Burgundy is a famous wine-growing region that stretches down to the city of Lyons, which the French consider to be the food capital of their country. Also known for its vineyards, the lush Loire Valley is home to thousands of magnificent châteaux, or castles.

Château de Chambord is a massive castle in the Loire Valley. It has 440 rooms and 13 staircases.

The Northwest

The long, windswept coastlines of Normandy and Brittany are dotted with sandy beaches and rugged cliffs. Inland, ancient villages date from medieval times. The Catholic saint Joan of Arc was burned at the stake in Rouen in 1431. William the Conqueror, who invaded England in 1066, is buried in Caen. Brittany's medieval ports, such as Brest and St. Nazaire, are known for fishing, shipbuilding, and sea trading. The port of St. Malo was once famous for pirates!

This is the Phare de Mean Ruz, a lighthouse on the Côte de Granit Rose (Pink Granite Coast) in Brittany.

A blue lake is surrounded by snowcapped mountains in the Pyrenees National Park.

Southern France

The Pyrenees Mountains separate France from Spain and Portugal. They stretch for 270 miles (434 km). The varied landscape ranges from dense forest to granite cliffs and snowcapped peaks. People visit the Pyrenees National Park to hike, climb, and see wild animals, such as brown bears and mountain goats.

Sun-drenched Provence is a region that attracts tourists with its stunning scenery and Mediterranean coastline. During summer vacation, Europeans head for the Cote d'Azur (in English, called the French Riviera) to relax and meet family and friends. For decades, towns such as Nice, Cannes, and St.Tropez have been fashionable places to swim, sunbathe—and be seen by others!

DID YOU KNOW?

A château is a castle or large house, and France has about 40,000 of them! Some are enormous, but others look like simple farmhouses. Any building on a vineyard estate can be called a château—whether it has castle turrets or not!

Food and Agriculture

Farming is important in France. The country leads the world in the production of dairy products. Each region has a wonderful variety of specialty foods.

The French are passionate about cheese, or *fromage*. From creamy varieties, such as Brie and Camembert, to hard cheeses like Cantal and Comté, they're included in many meals.

Northern Menu

France is famous for its dairy products. In Normandy, brown and white Normande cows produce the milk that goes into the region's world-famous cheeses. These include Camembert, Livarot, and Comté. The town of Isigny produces rich cream and butter— ingredients used in many local dishes.

Bread is eaten at most meals, so cereal crops are important. Wheat and buckwheat are grown In Brittany. Their flours are used to make *crêpes* and *gallettes* (a savory buckwheat crêpe). Brioche, a light, sweet roll, is another bakery specialty.

Most towns and villages in the countryside have a weekly market. This stand is selling fresh, local fruits.

MELON 5€50° les 2

Central Gardens

The Loire Valley is sometimes called the "Garden of France" because fruit and vegetables grow well in its rich soil. Pears and apples are grown in Anjou and Touraine. Vineyards in the Loire—and in the nearby regions of Rhône and Burgundy—produce some of the finest wines in the world. Almost half the mushrooms eaten in France are grown in limestone caves along the Loire River.

Charcuterie (cold cooked meats and sausages) are important to the French diet. Many of these products are made from animals that graze in the Dauphiné Alps and Savoyard. Charcuterie can be made from traditional pork and also from wild boar, chicken, and goose. Chicken reared in the town of Bresse (*poulet de Bresse*) is said to be the tastiest in the world!

Cows graze in a field in Normandy. Their milk is used to make the region's famous dairy foods.

Sunflowers are grown in southwestern France. The seeds are eaten or used to make oil.

Southern Fare

The Aquitaine region is famous for its poultry-based cuisine. Ducks and geese are bred to make *pâté*, duck breast, and goose gizzards. Duck and goose fat are used to add flavor to many dishes. The area is also known for its dairy farms and fruit orchards.

Walnut trees and sunflower crops are grown in Perigord and Quercy. The walnuts and sunflowers are used to make cooking oils.

Garlic is an important ingredient in French cuisine, and the Languedoc region grows some of the most flavorful. Languedoc is also known for its fine wines and delicious pitted fruits, such as peaches and apricots.

Coastal Catch

With hundreds of miles of coastline and five major rivers, it's not surprising that France has some of the best fish and seafood in Europe. Normandy is known for its huge catches of oysters and scallops. In Brittany, fresh crabs are caught near St. Malo, and Cameret is known for its lobsters. On the coast west of Bordeaux, all kinds of shellfish are caught. Freshwater fish, such as perch, salmon, and pike, are caught in the rivers of the Loire Valley. They are served fresh in local cuisine.

Honfleur is a picturesque fishing village on the French Normandy coast. Fishing boats unload their daily catch at its quayside.

Mediterranean Diet

The Mediterranean diet is one of the healthiest in the world. People who eat its vegetables, fish, pasta, and olive oil are said to live longer than those with more meat-heavy diets. In Provence, farmers grow garlic, peppers, tomatoes, eggplants, olives, and fennel.

Provence also has the perfect climate for growing herbs and scented lavender, used in cooking, cosmetics, and soaps.

Foods that make up the Mediterranean diet are healthiest when they are bought locally and eaten while they are fresh.

Let's Cook!

Cooking is a lot of fun! In this book, you will learn about different ingredients, which tastes go together, and new cooking methods. Some recipes have steps that you'll need help with, so you can ask a parent or another adult. When your delicious meal is ready, serve it up to family and friends!

Serves 4-6

This tells you how many people the meal will feed.

This lists all the ingredients you need for your meal.

Before you begin, check that you have everything. Get all the ingredients ready before you start cooking.

YOU WILL NEED

∗ 5 ounces milk chocolate or semisweet chocolate (or half of each)

∗ 2 large eggs

∗ 2 tablespoons powdered sugar

TOP TIP

You can choose any chocolate you like.

Top Tips give you more information about the recipe or the ingredients.

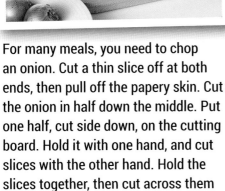

For many meals, you need to chop an onion. Cut a thin slice off at both ends, then pull off the papery skin. Cut the onion in half down the middle. Put one half, cut side down, on the cutting board. Hold it with one hand, and cut slices with the other hand. Hold the slices together, then cut across them to make small cubes. Be careful not to cut yourself!

Some recipes in this book use fresh garlic. Take a whole head of garlic. Break it into separate cloves. Cut the top and the bottom off each clove, then pull off the papery skin. You can chop the garlic clove with a sharp knife, or use a garlic press to crush the garlic directly into the skillet or saucepan.

METRIC CONVERSIONS

Oven Temperature			Liquid			Sugar	
°F	°C		cups	milliliters		cups	grams
275	140		¼	60		¼	50
300	150		½	120		½	100
325	170		¾	180		¾	150
350	180		1	240		1	200
375	190						
400	200		**Weight**			**Flour**	
425	220		ounces	grams		cups	grams
450	230		1	30		¼	30
475	240		2	60		½	60
			3	85		¾	90
			4	115		1	120
			5	140			
			6	175			
			7	200			
			8	225			

Alsace Onion Tart

Serves 6

This simple and delicious savory tart comes from the Alsace region, in eastern France. It can be eaten hot or cold, but it tastes great served hot with a salad.

YOU WILL NEED

FOR THE DOUGH

* 2 cups all-purpose flour
* ½ teaspoon salt
* 1 egg
* 1 ⅔ cups chilled butter

FOR THE TOPPING

* 1 pound 5 ounces onions
* 1 stick butter
* salt and pepper
* ½ teaspoon paprika
* 2 tablespoons flour
* 1 cup milk
* 2 egg yolks
* 1 cup heavy cream
* 4 ounces lean smoked ham
* 4 ounces Gruyère cheese

PLUS

* 1 quiche dish, 11 inches (28 cm) wide

1 Mix all the dough ingredients together. Knead, then shape into a ball. Wrap the dough in plastic wrap, then chill for 1 hour. Meanwhile, peel the onions, then cut them into very thin slices (see page 13). Separate the slices into rings.

2 Melt half the butter in a skillet. Add the onion rings and fry. Stir for 3 minutes, until they are golden. Season with salt, pepper, and paprika.

3 Put the rest of the butter in another skillet and melt it. Add the flour, stir, and fry until it's golden. Add milk, a little at a time, and keep stirring. Cook over low heat for about 5 minutes, then take the skillet off the heat. Stir in the egg yolks and cream. Finally, add the onions.

5 Spread the onion mixture onto the dough. Chop the ham into cubes and grate the cheese. Sprinkle both over the tart. Bake for 40 minutes. Leave it for 10 minutes before cutting.

4 Preheat the oven to 400°F. Knead the dough again, then roll it out thinly. Line the quiche dish with the dough. Cut off any dough that sticks over the top of the dish.

TOP TIP

Instead of making the dough yourself, you could use store-bought pastry. Choose puff pastry for a lighter crust.

Potato Gratin

Serves 3–4

Gratin dauphinois is from Grenoble, the capital of the Dauphiné region of France. Bake these tasty sliced potatoes until they are golden and crunchy.

YOU WILL NEED

* 1 pound waxy potatoes, such as Yukon Gold
* 2 garlic cloves
* 2 tablespoons butter (plus some more to grease the aluminum foil)
* 3 eggs
* 1⅔ cups heavy cream or milk
* salt and pepper
* parsley, to garnish (optional)

1 Preheat the oven to 400°F. Wash and peel the potatoes. Cut them into thin slices.

TOP TIP

Use potatoes that are about the same size so they take about the same time to cook.

2 Peel and chop the onion (see page 13). Melt the butter in a skillet until it foams. Fry the onion in the butter until it is transparent (see-through). Add the onion and butter to a gratin dish. Spread them around to grease the dish.

4 In a bowl, whisk the eggs with the cream or milk. Season with salt and pepper, then pour it over the potatoes.

5 Grease a sheet of aluminum foil with butter. Put the foil over the dish, then bake in the oven for about 20 minutes.

6 Remove the foil and continue baking for another 30 to 40 minutes, until the potatoes start to look golden brown. Check that the potatoes are cooked by pricking them with a sharp knife. They should feel almost soft.

3 Put the potato slices in the dish in overlapping circles.

Salade Niçoise

Serves 4

Fresh vegetables and sun-ripened tomatoes make this salad a tasty, healthy dish! The recipe and its name come from Nice, in southern France.

YOU WILL NEED

FOR THE SALAD

* ½ pound small potatoes
* 9 ounces green beans
* salt and pepper
* 1 red onion
* 4 tomatoes
* 1 small green bell pepper
* 1 can tuna in natural juice (6 ounces)
* ½ head of lettuce
* 4 eggs
* 10 black olives
* small bunch of basil

FOR THE DRESSING

* 4 tablespoons red wine vinegar
* 1 teaspoon mustard
* 1 garlic clove
* 6 tablespoons olive oil

1 Wash the potatoes, then boil them in their skins for about 15–20 minutes until they are slightly soft. Drain them and let them cool, then peel and slice them.

2 Wash the beans and trim off the tops and bottoms. Cook over low heat in salted water for 10 minutes. Drain, rinse under cold water, then drain them again in a colander.

3 Peel and halve the onion and slice thinly. Separate the slices. Wash the tomatoes and cut them into eighths. Discard the stem ends. Wash, trim, halve, and deseed the bell pepper. Cut it into strips.

4 Drain the tuna. Wash and dry the lettuce. Tear it into small pieces.

5 To make the dressing, whisk the vinegar and mustard. Crush and add the garlic. Whisk in the olive oil a little at a time until you have a creamy dressing.

6 Put all the vegetables into a serving bowl. Drizzle the dressing on top and toss together.

7 Boil four eggs for 8 minutes. When they're cold enough to touch, take off the shells. Cut each egg in half or into quarters. Add to the salad.

8 FInally, add the olives and the basil. Serve with crusty bread.

National Celebrations

France has 11 official national holidays every year. There are also many regional festivals for people to enjoy!

Bastille Day

Holidays

National holidays honor important events in France's history. Armistice Day (November 11) marks the end of World War I. Victory Day (May 8) remembers the end of World War II. About 85 percent of French people are Roman Catholic, so religious holidays and saints' days also have festivities and traditions.

Bastille Day is celebrated with a military parade in Paris.

A fireworks display lights up the sky above the Arc de Triomphe in Paris on Bastille Day.

Bastille Day

Bastille Day is a French national holiday celebrated throughout the country. It is also called *Quatorze Juillet* ("14th July"). Each year, the French remember July 14, 1789, when crowds stormed the Bastille prison in Paris. People were protesting against their uncaring king and queen, who had let people starve and live in poverty while they lived in luxury in grand palaces. This event sparked the French Revolution.

Like Independence Day (July 4) in the United States, Bastille Day is celebrated with firework displays, fairs, and family parties. In Paris, the French president leads a military parade, while airplanes fly in formation overhead.

DID YOU KNOW?

Since 1981, *Fête de la Musique* (World Music Day) has been celebrated on June 21. This is also the day when summer officially begins. In the streets, musicians play all kinds of music for free: rock, country, techno, rap, classical, and French songs.

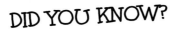

This *peloton*, or group of cyclists, rides up a flat road after the climb to Col de Manse in the Alps during a leg of Le Tour de France.

Touring France

The Tour de France is the world's greatest cycle race. It starts around the end of June each year and lasts for three weeks. Cyclists from around the world compete for the "Yellow Jersey," which is given to the winner. The race covers more than 2,200 miles (3,450 km) across flat, hilly, and mountainous regions in France. It sometimes visits nearby countries, too. Around 15 million people take time off work and school to gather at the roadside and cheer as the cyclists power past.

Saints' Day

The French celebrate *Toussaint*, or All Saints' Day, on November 1. This Catholic holiday honors relatives and friends who have died, as well as saints who have no special day. After attending church services, people place chrysanthemum flowers on the graves of loved ones. Children carve jack-o'-lanterns with scary faces and trick or treat, just as they do in the United States on Halloween.

A jack-o'-lantern and decorated cupcakes are part of a Toussaint celebration.

Festival of Lights

The Lyon Festival of Lights is a four-day event that starts on December 8. It was first celebrated in 1852. The people of Lyon set up a statue of the Virgin Mary on a hilltop and were saved from a terrible storm. Today, brightly colored light shows turn the city's famous buildings into a spectacular display.

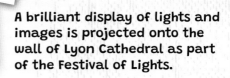

A brilliant display of lights and images is projected onto the wall of Lyon Cathedral as part of the Festival of Lights.

Méchoui

Serves 4-6

This dish is originally from North Africa. Méchoui means "barbecued lamb." At village celebrations, a whole lamb is roasted on a spit. This is the smaller, family-size version!

YOU WILL NEED

* 1 handful of fresh mint
* 4 garlic cloves, plus extras
* 2 tablespoons paprika
* 3 teaspoons ground cumin
* 4 tablespoons sunflower oil or butter
* 1 small leg of lamb (about 5–6 pounds)
* salt and ground cumin for sprinkling
* rosemary sprigs, to garnish

1 First, wash the mint stalks and shake them dry. Pull off the leaves and chop them very finely. Peel the garlic and put it through a garlic press.

2 In a large bowl, stir the mint, garlic, paprika, cumin, and oil to make a smooth paste.

4 Preheat the oven to 380°F. Add a few cloves of garlic around the meat. Cook the lamb in the oven for about 2–2½ hours, depending on its size.

5 The meat should be tender enough to pull off the bone (but don't touch the meat until it has cooled a little). Sprinkle the roast with salt and cumin. Garnish with rosemary sprigs and serve.

3 Place the lamb in the bowl and brush the paste all over it. Then put the meat in a roasting dish and cover it with a clean kitchen cloth. Leave it to marinate for at least 1 hour.

DID YOU KNOW?

In North Africa, the lamb is traditionally cooked over a fire hole or pit in the ground.

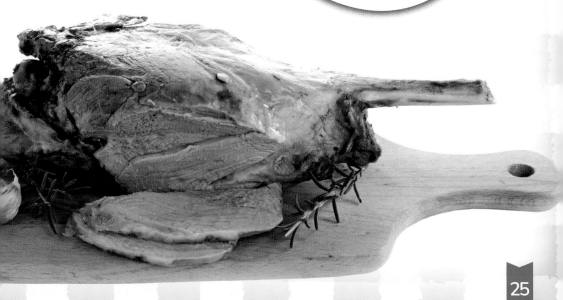

Crêpes Suzette

Makes 8 crêpes

Crêpes are a specialty of Brittany and northern France. They can be made with different fillings, but this crêpe has a sauce of caramelized sugar, butter, and oranges.

YOU WILL NEED

FOR THE CRÊPES

* 2 eggs
* 1 cup milk
* ¾ cup all-purpose flour
* 1 tablespoon sugar
* 2 tablespoons unsalted butter

FOR THE SAUCE

* 3 large oranges
* ¼ cup sugar
* 2 tablespoons unsalted butter

1 Put the eggs, milk, flour, and sugar in a bowl. Stir for 3 minutes to make a thin batter. Melt the butter in a small skillet until it is golden brown, and stir it into the mixture. Set the batter aside.

2 Scrub the oranges under hot water, then pat them dry. Squeeze out $3/4$ cup of juice. Simmer the juice and sugar in a saucepan over medium heat, stirring until the sugar is melted. Add the butter half a tablespoon at a time, stirring constantly.

DID YOU KNOW?

A crêpe is a pancake that is much thinner than an American pancake. Sweet crêpes can be filled with apples, berries, or preserves. Savory crêpes may have ham, cheese, or mushroom fillings.

3 Peel the remaining orange, completely removing the white piths (inner skins). With a sharp knife, cut out the orange slices between their thin skins.

4 Melt some of the butter in a nonstick skillet until it foams. Pour in 1 ladleful of batter. Turn the skillet so that the batter covers the whole base. Fry the crêpe for 1 minute. Turn it over with a spatula, and fry the other side for about 30 seconds.

5 Put the finished crêpe on a rack or a large plate, and cover it with a clean cloth. Fry seven more crêpes.

6 Put a few orange slices on each crêpe, and fold the crêpe over to form a small triangle. Put the crêpes back into the skillet, one at a time, and pour a little of the syrup over the top. Heat for 1 minute and serve.

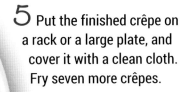

Family Celebrations

French people love to celebrate at home. They prepare special food for important days, such as Christmas, New Year's Day, a wedding, or a birthday.

The French often invite family or friends over for lunch or dinner. Meals are an important way for everyone to spend time together.

Slow Food

The French believe in taking their time to enjoy food over talk with family and friends. Traditionally, lunch and dinner have been opportunities for families to gather for a long and leisurely two-hour meal. Today, this is not always possible, but people keep the tradition whenever they can. Meal courses include *hors d'oeuvres*, or appetizers; a soup course; charcuterie; a fish dish; and a roast meat or stew. Unlike in the United States, vegetables and salad are served after the main dish! Cheeses round off the feast, followed by a dessert such as *tarte Tatin*, a kind of apple tart.

Christmas Eve

On Christmas Eve, people prepare a special late meal. Then they go to church for midnight mass—a service that celebrates the birth of Christ on Christmas Day (December 25). Traditional carols are sung in the church, which is often lit with a blaze of candles. Back at home, Père Noël ("Father Christmas," or Santa Claus) leaves gifts for the children in shoes, stockings, or next to the tree. Many French homes set up a little *crèche* (Nativity scene) showing the baby Jesus in a manger with Mary and Joseph. The whole family helps make this.

This is the Galeries LaFayette in Paris. Every year, a huge Christmas tree is hung beneath the building's magnificent glass dome.

This *croquembouche* wedding cake is decorated with flowers and threads of caramel.

Weddings

Traditionally, people in France get married in a church or chapel. Before the ceremony, the groom meets the bride at her home, and they walk to the church. Children block their way by holding up white ribbons, which the bride must cut with scissors. This symbolizes breaking through obstacles in life. At the ceremony, the groom walks his mother down the aisle as a sign of respect. Then, at the reception, the bride and groom lean over a cake called a croquembouche ("crunches in the mouth"). This is a cone of *profiteroles* (cream-filled pastries). If they can kiss without knocking the cake over, they will have a long and happy life together!

People give each other sprays of lily of the valley on May 1. In the language of flowers, lily of the valley means "return of happiness."

Mother's Day

The French tradition of Mother's Day is said to have started in 1806, when emperor Napoleon Bonaparte announced a special day for children to honor their mothers. Today, people give their mothers chocolates, flowers, cakes, and original poems. They may also treat their mom to a special meal, whether home-cooked or at a nice restaurant.

Crowds of people dressed in red and white gather at the five-day summer festival of Bayonne (Fêtes de Bayonne).

French Fêtes

Every area of France has its own *fête*, or festival, that celebrates the harvest or another important event. Traditionally, people in rural areas contribute to the occasion by making food and bringing drinks for a big, communal meal.

Today, even though many people work in industries other than farming, the custom continues. Sometimes hundreds of people gather for a meal. The fête can last for days, with music, dancing, local crafts—and even more food!

31

Duck Breast

Serves 4

This is a classic dish from southwestern France. People like to serve it on special occasions, such as birthdays. It's easy to cook and tastes delicious!

YOU WILL NEED

* ✳ 3 tablespoons lemon juice
* ✳ 2 tablespoons honey
* ✳ salt and pepper
* ✳ 2 duck breast fillets (about 10 ounces each)
* ✳ 2 tablespoons olive oil
* ✳ a handful of shallots, diced
* ✳ scallion slices, to garnish

1 Put the lemon juice, honey, salt, and pepper in a bowl and stir. Wash the duck breasts under cold water, and pat them dry. Put them in a large ovenproof dish, then rub all over with the marinade. Cover the dish with plastic wrap and chill for 2 hours.

TOP TIP

You can also cook duck in an oven preheated to 400°F. Prick the skin with a fork. Place on a rack, skin side down, and put a baking dish underneath to catch drippings. Roast for 20–30 minutes.

2 Remove the duck breast fillets from the marinade and pat them dry. Set the marinade aside. Preheat the oven to 200°F.

3 Heat the oil over medium heat in a skillet. Put the fillets in, skin side down, and fry them for about 7 minutes. Turn them over and fry for another 5–7 minutes.

4 Place the duck breasts on a serving platter and cover. Put them in a warm preheated oven.

5 Peel and slice the shallots. Fry them in the skillet over medium heat until they look see-through. Add 5 tablespoons water. Using a wooden spoon, loosen the meat juices in the skillet. Add the marinade, and bring the sauce to a boil. Season with salt and pepper.

6 Cut the duck breast into slices. Arrange the slices on a platter and pour some sauce over the top. Scatter the scallion slices around.

Chocolate Mousse

Serves 4-6

Chocolate mousse is a popular dessert. Make this delicious, creamy dish for a party, birthday, or other celebration.

YOU WILL NEED

* ✱ 5 ounces milk chocolate or semisweet chocolate (or half of each)
* ✱ 2 large eggs
* ✱ 2 tablespoons powdered sugar
* ✱ ½ cup heavy cream
* ✱ 1 teaspoon vanilla extract
* ✱ whipped cream and chocolate crumbs, to serve

1 Chop or break the chocolate into medium-size pieces, then put them into a small bowl.

2 Put some water in a saucepan that is slightly larger than the bowl, and bring the water to a simmer.

TOP TIP

You can choose any chocolate you like. Try making the mousse with white chocolate, or chocolate flavored with orange or mint.

3 Put the bowl in the saucepan and stir the chocolate continuously as it melts. Take the pan off the heat.

5 In a large bowl, whisk the egg yolks and the vanilla extract together until they are creamy. Add the melted chocolate, stirring the mixture continuously.

6 Put the whipped cream on top of the chocolate mixture. Gently stir it in with a whisk or rubber spatula.

4 Separate the egg whites from the yolks. Using a whisk, beat the egg whites until they are stiff. Slowly sprinkle in the sugar while you whisk, then chill the egg whites in the refrigerator. Whip the cream and put it in the refrigerator to chill.

7 Now put the stiff egg whites on top. Very gently, stir them into the mixture with a metal spoon. Don't mix or whisk, or the mousse will collapse.

8 Chill the mousse in the refrigerator for at least 3 hours. Spoon it into serving glasses and decorate with a little whipped cream and chocolate crumbs.

Life in France

Like most people in Western Europe, French people live in cities, towns, villages, or on farms and vineyards. When they are not working, they enjoy sports, games, and summer vacations!

The Pull of Paris

Life in big cities such as Paris, Lyon, and Marseilles can be crowded and busy. In Paris, the capital of France, people commute (travel daily) into town from the surrounding suburbs. Many ride the bus or the Métro, a train system with more than 300 stations. Stores, galleries, and office buildings line the wide boulevards of Paris. People eat at cafés and restaurants, which serve French and other cuisines. They also buy delicious fresh bread, pastries, and cakes at *boulangeries*, or bakeries.

Paris is a bustling capital city known for its cafés, shops, museums, and historical sites. This is the famous Louvre Museum.

Many families get away from the cities in August and go camping in the countryside.

Taking a Break

The French treasure their vacation time, when they can get away from daily life and relax with the family. Most people have five weeks' vacation from work a year. Traditionally, the French take off the whole month of August and head for a beautiful spot.

The coastal towns along the French Riviera are popular destinations. Other favorite places are lake resorts and the mountains. Some people have their own summer homes in the country, and some stay with friends. Camping out under the stars is popular, too, since French summers are generally warm. People may also vacation in other countries, such as Italy, Austria, Switzerland, Spain, the United Kingdom, or the United States.

DID YOU KNOW?

Paris is the most densely populated city in Europe. Plus, around 30 million tourists roam through its streets sightseeing each year!

People have fun swimming and relaxing on a beach at Annecy Lake. It is one of the most popular resorts in France.

Sport

Football ("soccer" in the United States) is a huge sport in France. People follow their local and national teams, and games between rival teams are big events. Rugby is another favorite team sport. The French also enjoy individual sports such as sailing, fencing, car racing, and tennis.

People take advantage of France's varied landscape. They swim in lakes and rivers, sail along the coast, and go fishing, hiking, rock climbing, and spelunking inland. Skiing and mountain climbing in the Alps and Pyrenees Mountains are also popular activities.

Pétanque is a game that started in Provence. It traditionally uses silver steel balls, but *boules*, a popular beach version of the game, is played with colored plastic balls.

School Days

Education starts early in France. In many families, both parents work, so babies and toddlers go to daycare centers during the week. Young children go to *maternelle*, or preschool. This is a chance for them to interact with other children and learn social skills. Elementary school starts at six years old. Children learn writing, math, history, and geography. From 11 to 14 years old, children go to *collège*, where languages and computers are studied, too. Next comes the *lycée*, where students take *le Bac*, a hard exam. When they pass, it's like graduating from high school.

However, it's not all hard work. Schoolchildren often go on class trips to museums and historic places. At palaces such as Versailles, they learn how kings and queens lived. At the Louvre, they see some of the world's most famous paintings.

 French schoolchildren visit the medieval castle in the city of Carcassonne. The old part of the city is a UNESCO World Heritage Site.

French Onion Soup

Serves 6

This popular everyday soup is unbelievably yummy! People in France often grow their own onions, which give this soup a country-fresh flavor.

YOU WILL NEED

* ✳ 2 large white onions
* ✳ 2 tablespoons duck or goose fat
* ✳ 4 ounces Cantal cheese or Monterey Jack cheese
* ✳ 4 ounces Gruyère cheese
* ✳ French bread, a day or two old and a little stale
* ✳ salt and pepper

1 Peel and chop the onions. Put the duck fat into a large saucepan and heat it over medium heat. Now add the onions. Fry them over low heat until they are a golden color. Keep stirring as you fry them so they don't stick to the pan.

2 Put about 2–2½ quarts water in the saucepan. Season the soup with salt and pepper. Cover the saucepan with a lid, and simmer the soup over low heat for 25 minutes.

TOP TIP

This soup is usually made with Cantal cheese, from the French Auvergne region. It has a strong, earthy flavor. Gruyère is tangy and great for melting.

3 Using a large-holed grater, grate both cheeses. Slice the bread into thin slices, and preheat the oven broiler.

4 Put a layer of bread and a layer of cheese into ovenproof soup bowls. Pour the soup over it, then top with the rest of the cheese and bread.

5 Place the bowls under the broiler for about 5 minutes, until the cheese melts. Using oven mitts, put the bowls on heatproof dishes and serve.

40-Clove Chicken

Serves 4

This is a classic French recipe. Don't be put off by 40 cloves of garlic! As it cooks, the strong, tangy flavor of garlic becomes mild, while the clove turns soft and buttery.

YOU WILL NEED

* ✳ 1 large chicken (about 3½ pounds)
* ✳ salt and pepper
* ✳ ½ bunch parsley
* ✳ few sprigs of thyme
* ✳ 40 garlic cloves (3–4 heads)
* ✳ 2 bay leaves
* ✳ ½ lemon
* ✳ 4 tablespoons olive oil
* ✳ 1–2 cups chicken broth
* ✳ ½ bunch dill, to garnish

1 Preheat the oven to 450°F. Season the chicken inside and out with salt and pepper. Rinse the parsley and thyme, and tear the leaves off the stalks. Peel and roughly chop four of the garlic cloves.

SAFETY TIP

Always wash your hands with soap and warm water after handling raw chicken. Use different cutting boards and utensils for meat and produce.

2 Push the chopped garlic, parsley, thyme, bay leaves, and the half lemon into the chicken cavity.

3 Pour the oil into a large cooking pot. Add the chicken and turn it in the oil to coat. Leave the chicken in the pot breast side down.

5 Turn the chicken over, and pour the chicken broth into the pot. Roast for another 30–40 minutes or until the chicken is completely cooked.

6 Check to see if the chicken is cooked. Prick the fattest part of a leg with a skewer and then pull it out. If the juices are pink, the chicken needs more cooking. If they are clear, it is done. Garnish with the dill, and serve with the roasted garlic.

4 Wash the remaining garlic heads with their skin on. Then cut each head in half (or separate out the cloves), and place them next to the chicken. Roast the chicken and garlic for 30 minutes.

Tarte Tatin

Makes 1 tart

This upside-down apple tart originated in France but is now made worldwide! It is delicious hot, straight from the oven. Serve it with cream or ice cream.

YOU WILL NEED

* ⅔ cup chilled butter
* 1⅛ cups all-purpose flour (plus more for the work surface)
* 1 pinch baking powder
* 2 tablespoons sugar
* 1 pinch salt
* 1 egg yolk
* 2¼ pounds Golden Delicious apples
* 1⅛ cups powdered sugar

PLUS

* ovenproof pie plate, 11 inches (28 cm) in diameter

1 Cut ¼ cup butter into cubes. Mix the butter, flour, baking powder, sugar, salt, and egg yolk to make a smooth dough. Shape into a ball. Cover in plastic wrap, and chill for 1 hour.

2 Preheat the oven to 450°F. Peel and quarter the apples, cutting out the cores. Sprinkle the base of the pie plate with powdered sugar. Bake in the center of the oven for 10 minutes, until the sugar turns a golden caramel color. Put the rest of the butter in the plate and let it melt.

DID YOU KNOW?

This tart was invented by mistake by the Tatin sisters, who worked in a hotel in France. They were busy and forgot to put the dough into the plate first when they were making an apple tart.

3 Lay out the apple pieces, with the rounded side down, on top of the caramel. Bake for about 5 minutes in the center of the oven.

4 Next, lightly flour your work surface and roll out the dough. Make a circle a little larger than the pie plate. Take the pie plate out of the oven, and turn the heat down to 400°F.

5 Using a rolling pin to help, lift the dough over the apples. Press it down lightly around the edges, and prick the top several times with a fork. Bake the tart for about 30 minutes.

6 Ask your assistant to help with this step. First, take the tart out of the oven. Put a large round platter on top, then quickly turn over both pie plate and platter, holding them together tightly. Remove the pie plate and serve.

Glossary

Armistice Day (November 11)
A national holiday that celebrates the end of World War I in 1918.

Bastille Day (July 14) A national holiday that celebrates the storming of the Bastille prison in Paris on July 14, 1789. It sparked the French Revolution.

boulangerie A bakery that sells fresh bread, cakes, and pastries.

charcuterie Cold cooked meats. A charcuterie board often includes cheese along with these meats.

crêpe suzette A sweet pancake from northern France.

croquembouche A French wedding cake that is a tall pyramid made of stacked cream-filled pastries. It is often decorated with caramel threads and fresh flowers.

French Revolution (1789–1799)
A civil war that brought about major changes in the way France is governed. People rebelled against the king and queen.

gratin A dish made with cheese or cream. It is baked in the oven so a crunchy crust forms.

le Bac An exam that students take before they graduate from the French equivalent of high school.

marinate The process of soaking foods in a liquid (marinade) before cooking.

méchoui A North African dish of whole marinated and roasted or barbecued lamb.

pétanque A popular French game played with metal balls.

tarte Tatin An upside-down tart with caramelized apples that comes from central France. It is named after the Tatin sisters, who came up with the recipe.

Tour de France An annual French bicycle race that lasts for three weeks. The race takes place on flat, hilly, and mountainous areas.

Toussaint (November 1)
Toussaint (All Saints' Day) is celebrated by visiting the graves of family members who have died.

Victory Day (May 8) A day that celebrates France's freedom from German rule at the end of World War II in 1945.

Further Resources

Books

GoldInk Books.
French Bread Baking for Kids.
GoldInk Books, 2021.

Halperin, Shira.
Kids' Travel Guide France & Paris.
Flying Kids, 2016.

Michels, Mardi.
French Food for Everyone: Le Goûter (After School Snacks).
MLM Publications, 2021.

Michels, Mardi.
In the French Kitchen with Kids: Easy, Everyday Dishes for the Whole Family to Make and Enjoy.
Random House, 2018.

Pepin, Claudine.
Let's Cook French, A Family Cookbook.
Quarry Books, 2021.

Websites

www.kids-world-travel-guide.com/food-in-france.html
Pages with French recipes and links to French facts and maps.
blog.dinolingo.com/category/french-culture-for-kids/
Page with links to French history, food, customs, and landmarks.
www.natgeokids.com/uk/discover/geography/countries/facts-about-france/
Facts about France from National Geographic Kids.
kids.kiddle.co/France
All about France, its history, geography, culture, and food, with numerous links.

Publisher's note to educators and parents: Our editors have carefully reviewed these websites to ensure that they are suitable for students. Many websites change frequently, however, and we cannot guarantee that a site's future contents will continue to meet our high standards of quality and educational value. Be advised that students should be closely supervised whenever they access the Internet.

Index